Ice Goes Out

by
Danl Lane

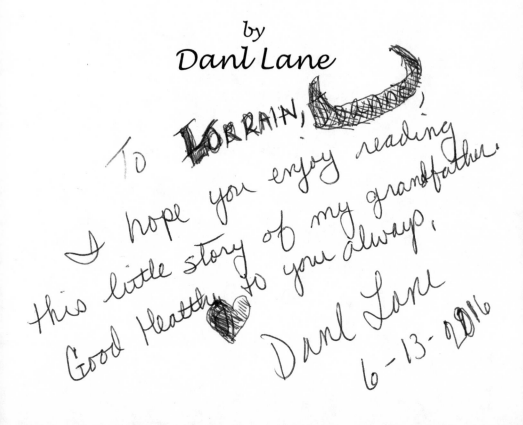

To LORRAIN,

I hope you enjoy reading
this little story of my grandfather.
Good Health to you always,

Danl Lane
6-13-2016

This book is a work of fiction. Places, events, and situations in this story are purely fictional. Any resemblance to actual persons, living or dead, is coincidental.

First published by AuthorHouse 04/29/04

ISBN: 1-4184-5992-5 (e-book)
ISBN: 1-4184-4284-4 (Paperback)

This book is printed on acid free paper.

This book was written in memory
of Chief Tomekin, Leslie Ranco.

Many thanks to Valentine Ranco, June Rain Ranco,
Charlie and Eileen Dahill, Leroy Lane, Carol Lane and
the Penobscot Nation.

Table of Contents

He died penniless selling his pencils in Boston. How could this be? How could the kindest, most generous, thoughtful most smart, bravest most loyal, hardest working, friend to all, die a poor man?

Well, it happened.

Everyone on the streets from Boston to Bangor knew of Johnny Boyle. They knew of his Irish immigrant parents who lived in Boston. They knew of his Penobscot Indian girlfriend, Ada, who lived on Indian Island Reservation with her parents in Old Town, Maine. They knew that Johnny Boyle would only go to work for the highest bidder amongst the big three northern paper companies and bid they did. The big monopolies owned the land, they owned the saw mills and paper mills, and they owned the strongest men in the east. They didn't own Johnny. They needed Johnny and he knew it. Down east residents knew when a logging season began and when it ended. They knew when paydays came, especially the street bums, knowing if they begged JB for a nickel, they would get an actual dollar, each and every one of them.

What most did not know is where Johnny learned how to cook, and cook he could. He was only the best in New England. Lumberjacks from Calais to Kathadin knew of his reputation. His meals were unmatched. The lumberjacks would travel miles out of their way, looking for the camp that hired Johnny. He would serve four voracious meals a day. After all, the logging business was tough, tough work. The better fed, the longer the men could endure. The big three knew this all too well, which is what made Johnny invaluable to them.

MaCarthy Boyle, Johnny's dad, taught his son everything. During hard times, Mac would take Johnny along on hunting trips in the deep woods of Maine. Mac would bring back enough meat for his entire Boston neighborhood, friends, and family. The fresh game would be already cut into the finest steaks and chops, poultry parts and grounded hamburg as well. All this was done in the woods, while little Johnny watched. He was fascinated by his dads' quick knife. Mac knew right where to cut, skin, strip, scrape, salt, de-bone, filet...it was quite remarkable.

They learned to survive out there. He watched his dad get a frying pan scorching hot, "That is the key, JB," he used to say, and promptly spit on it. Mac would grill two moose steaks to perfection. Juicy, tender, melt in your mouth, cut it with a fork…. all of those. Breakfast was just as scrumptous…eggs, squirrel meat, fish…all to die for. He was taught to make jerky and nothing was wasted. Johnny learned.

Johnny was so appreciative he named his huge wood stove 'Black Mac', after his dad. His stove was as much of a legend as Johnny himself. It was the size of a small pool table and he'd haul it to any location, any campsite, any mountain. It would arrive from Boston by pick up truck and he would hire a team of whoever was around to get the damn thing on tobaggans. If there was no snow he'd haul it right over the leaves. Some said it was a good thing that Johnny did not play the piano. He'd harness himself and his team of men to the tobaggans and pull through the woods, sometimes making paths and new roads as they went, all along gently treating his stove like a family of three. It was his livelihood. If he were lucky, there would be a dingle or wongon, a dining hut already erected. All the camps had bunkhouses where the axe men slept. Sometimes he'd put together a makeshift tin kitchen and cook in the great outdoors. He chose a spot, carefully leveled it, plucked down his stove

and began to clean, shine, scrub and bathe 'Black Mac' till it shone and sparkled. He would buff 'Black Mac' night after night, right through the entire logging season, from day one till the ice goes out.

Most of the lumberjacks would wonder how 'Black Mac' ever got to some of the remotest timberlands in the northeast. It was no secret to JB. He was usually set up a full week in advance, even before the first horses were stabled in the hovel. He knew a little cash would go a long way if you hired the right individuals. He was a young 35, and not a very big built man. He was more like Abe Lincoln, just not as tall. The muscles he developed came from chopping firewood to fuel Black Mac, not from using a ripsaw, felling a giant oak, or working a log drive down river. I don't think he ever used a pick pole or a cantdog nor did he ever dynamite a wing. No, he didn't have that experience. He was experienced in two things; cooking and hiring help. He could handle the cooking, but he relied heavily on the men he hired. He would pay them well, but more important to him, he would feed them well.

Johnny Boyle would sometimes hire the Penobscots and Passamaquoddys. He knew their lives were one of strife and turmoil. This is how he met Ada.

Ada, a Penobscot herself; the dear girl took care of her parents on the reservation and they lived comfortably in a small cabin. Her place was the first after the bridge and right on the Penobscot River. Most of the family housing on the reservation was rather poor... falling down shacks in desperate need of repair, leaky roofs, broken fences, rusting heaps of automobiles in every other yard. There were some nice homes with neat and trimmed yards, but far and few in between. To say the least, Adas was one of the nicer cabins and most of that had to do with Johnny. He really loved the people, not just the Penobscots, but most people. I know. I lived down the dead end street across from Adas'. My name is Leslie and I was only a boy of fourteen when Johnnie first hired me to be his cookee. It happened right after Christmas on one of Johnny's routine visits to Ada before he headed off into the woods for the next most unforgettable three and a half months.

CHAPTER 2

That evening, I was standing on the bridge that connected the island to Old Town. It was December 31, the last day of 1929, and a balmy 22 degrees. A light dusting of snow had fallen earlier and it dotted the land like powdered cookies.

Seymour Wiggins, the government guy, drove buy in his government car and was drunk already. He was fat, in his 50's and unfriendly, a real scrooge type, which made me surprised to hear him holler out the window, "Happy New Year", as he swerved back and forth across the bridge. He was probably leaving because he caught wind that Johnny Boyle would soon be arriving. Seymour Wiggins and Johnny Boyle did not get along. Wiggins had a small office on the island that was really the reservations fire station. It had one long hose and a pump on wheels that would be drawn by horses to any serious fire. The pump would draw water from the river and everybody on the reservation would man the hose. Everybody except Wiggins. He would say his only job was being in charge of handing out the surplus food and finding the men jobs for the WPA, jobs created by the government because times were tough.

I leaned over the railing to see if any of my rocks could break through the ice that formed on the Penobscot River. It was already solid and would be safe for our annual New

Years Day Skating Festival. Solid, except for the open water and rapids upstream. That never froze, unless it got really cold for a period of weeks.

It was about sunset and I could see from across the bay the workers leaving the Breyhausser Paper Mill, one of three mills the company owned. They would shut down for the weekend holiday.

Ada had tipped me off that Johnny would be arriving about 5 p.m. with his pick up truck and 'Black Mac' in tow. Like clockwork, I could see him bouncing in his cab as he turned on to the bridge. I started running towards Ada's announcing at the top of my lungs, "Johnnys' coming."

Johnny and I had a few things in common. Although I was Penobscot and he was an Irishman, alcohol took its toll on both ancestors and heritage. Johnny's parents both died of alcohol poisoning and it bothered him good. 'Firewater' ran rampant throughout our reservation, too, destroying many lives and families. I was one of the fortunate ones. Rarely, neither of my parents drank. My father, Joseph, and mother, Emma, always stuck close to traditions. Occasionally, they still spoke the language, as broken as it was. Like Johnny, my father showed me how to do many things. He taught me hunting, archery, smoking meat and fish, the craft of sewing moccasins and carving war clubs. As an elder, he grew more into the politics of the Penobscot Nation and I didn't see much of him after that. Mom would still make dinner every night with leftovers, deer meat and what government food we could scrape up. However, she always managed to give us a dessert, even if it was only molasses on bread. She still did a lot of canning and she would spend her time making sweet grass baskets, doing beadwork, and making porcupine quill jewelry, all to sell to the summer tourists. I could sense she was slowing down, and starting to forget a lot. She totally forgot my last birthday. I probably would have forgotten about it myself if it had not been for Johnny Boyle. He gave me a rabbit pelt with "Happy Birthday, Les, from J.B.," scratched into the back of the skin.

"Johnnys coming! Johnnys coming!" I yelled. He always had something for everyone.

A few kids gathered at Adas' driveway and she herself look out her window. Johnnys' truck rumbled into the drive way. He shut off the engine and the truck coughed once as he got out.

"Hello, Les...how's things?"...he smiled. I liked being the first one he greeted.

"Hi Val, Dana, June,"...he knew everyones name. He made his way to the back of the truck to secure the ropes that were binding 'Black Mac'.

"Whad't ya bring us ? Whad't ya bring us?"...the kids said in harmony.

"Oh, sorry, nothing this time,"...he liked to tease, and no sooner did he say that when he jumped up onto 'Black Mac', opened a lid and pulled out boxes and boxes of taffy.

"Fresh taffy for everyone! Right from New York! Here you go," and started tossing the boxes to a small crowd that collected.

"Hey Johnny, the big three are in town," one voice could be heard.

"I'm sure they'll find me," Johnny replied.

"Are you skating tomorrow, JB?" another one asked.

"Not sure yet," JB said, "Let me go in and check with Ada and see if she'll give me permission." Everyone chuckled and looked at each other as he grabbed a suitcase and a box of taffy and disappeared into the house.

Ada had made some cookies and had hot tea for JB. She was about 3 years younger than Johnny, or 32, I guess, and of medium build. She was a fine cook herself and just as hospitable. Her short sandy hair was curled into the style of that year and though she was not overly beautiful, her generosity made up for it. She had one of the few homes that housed a piano, and sat through many sour notes as she let the nuns teach students in her home.

"Hi, my love. This is for you," handing her the taffy. "Is this for me?" Johnny inquired sniffing at the fresh baked cookies.

"Yes it is," replied Ada, "but don't eat it all at once. I want to save some for skating tomorrow."

"Where's my kiss from the women who slaved all day?" Johnny implied.

Ada embraced Johnny and gave him a peck on the lips.

"Why are you filling those kid minds with tall tales?" Ada asked.

"Whatever do you mean?" replied JB.

"Telling them this taffy is fresh from New York!"

"Well, it is fresh!" defended Johnny.

"Yeah, but it says York, Maine on the box," points Ada. "Not New York!"

"Well, it was my first time passing through York so it was new to me. Right!" Johnny snickered.

Ada sneered, "Oh! Johnny, I missed you. Mother has not been feeling well and Dads out getting medicine."

"Oh?"

Ada continued, "and the Big Three have been here for three days scouting out the place. One of them even had the nerve to walk right up and look in my window."

"And did you give a good show?" joked JB. Ada slaps his jacket and returned to doing her dishes.

"Well, I'll have a talk with them. I'm sure we'll negotiate and I'll sign a contract down on the ice tomorrow." Are you going skating?"

"Maybe for a little while," replied Ada, "I don't want to leave mom for too long if she's not feeling better."

Just then, the door swung open and Adas' dad, Wilton, in red hunting clothes, bursts in with an armful of firewood. He was a stalky build and had a head of thick, dark hair with a beaded headband. He was still quite strong and active for a man in his 60's.

"Hey Johnny," he cried.

"Hey, Will...let me help you with that," Johnny offered. They stacked the wood by the pot-bellied stove.

"Johnny, did they tell you the Big Three are here already?" asked Wilton.

"Well, I've heard." said Johnny.

9

"They're talking of a pretty good stand of timber this year," he continued. "Georgia Pacific bought 1500 acres on the stump in Machias, and Breyhausser bought Township #31 from Great Northern. I think Great Northern is hurting this year so I would only deal with the other two."

"Gosh, Will, you've really been doing your homework," implied JB.

"Not really. I overheard them down at Marie's Chat & Chew. I just got big ears," explained Bill.

A faint voice was heard calling from the backroom. "Ada, is that Johnny?"

"Ah, yes it is mom," and she loudly whispered to her father "Dad, did you bring the medicine?"

"Oh! No, I didn't have enough money,"...dropping his eyes.

"Dad!" Ada replied sternly.

"Send him here!" the faint voice commanded. Ada looked at Johnny and he shrugged, obliged, and slipped into the backroom. Johnny entered the dim but well heated room and saw Doe, short for Dorothy, well tucked into her Indian blankets.

"How you feeling?" JB sympathized.

The mom was a frail woman but had an ever-piercing Indian glare. Her long graying hair was once jet black and you could tell she was a beautiful Indian princess in her younger days. JB knelt beside her and she spoke her law softly.

"Now look, Johnny. I do not want you taking the first offer they give you. Understand? You hold out."

"Oh yes, Doe," Johnny responded agreeably as she went on with her list of demands.

"And this year, tell them you want traveling expenses to and from the Penobscot Exchange. (cough)

You use your truck for them, bringing them all that produce and supplies. Tell them you want compensation! Compensation," she repeated.

"Good idea, mama, I'll do that. Now you rest and you get better," JB assured her as he quietly left the room and closed the door.

"And tell them you want a new truck! Yours sounds awful!" as one last request could be faintly heard.

Johnny re-entered the room wide-eyed.

"C'mon," commanded Johnny to Will, "hop in old Betsy outside and we'll go get that medicine. We'll have time to catch up."...

"Let's go. I'm with ya," said Will.

The two hopped into the truck and rode off.

CHAPTER 3

New Years Days turned out to be a perfect skating day with temperatures around 28 and the sun shining brightly. Plenty of people came out to skate, play in the games and have cider and donuts, hot coffee and tea. Johnny made his way down to the ice and sat on the dock next to Val, his favorite little 7 year old Penobscot girl.

"How's my doll? Aren't you skating today?"

"Maybe," Val answered.

"Val!" he pondered out loud. "Gee, that's such a lovely name. How did your parents come up with that?"

"You know, Johnny... February 14th... when I was born!"

"Oh, I keep forgetting. Halloween, right?" Johnny joked.

"SSShhhh...Johnny...," she hushed him putting her finger to her lips.

"I want to hear what these girls are fighting about..."

While Johnny finished lacing his skates, he and Val overheard the conversation of three 13-year-old girls.

"...and you won't be able to come over my house anymore and if you don't want to be my best friend, I will never, ever let you use my brand new skates I got for Christmas," the tall, skinny one quipped.

"Aw, go on and keep your stupid skates Mary Lou," said one girl.

"Yeah, we wouldn't be your friend for $100 dollars," said the other. "We don't care if we ever go over to your stupid house. We don't care if we ever see you again," ...and with that, the two girls stormed off.

JB was watching Val's reaction and was so surprised to see her jump up and meekly say, "Mary Lou, I'll be your friend," while never taking her eyes off the new sparkling skates.

Mary Lou replied, "You! Well... alright... I guess. Just for today. Where are your skates? Didn't you get a new pair for Christmas too?"

"Well, I did, but ... but... I forgot them," Val said hesitating and continued, "Can I try yours? I am your new best friend!"

"They won't fit you. My foot is almost three sizes bigger than yours," Mary Lou exclaimed.

Without missing a beat, Val got up and ran to the nearest outhouse. In a flash she was back with a Sears Catalog in one hand and a ball of toilet paper in the other. She smiled at Mary Lou and held up her find.

"This'll work," she said. Mary Lou had to be astonished and gave in.

"All right," she responded as she rolled her eyes and shook her head. She sat down to unlace her skates as Val tore some pages out of the catalog and began crumpling them with the toilet paper. No sooner had Mary Lou taken off one skate when Val had it stuffed to size 3. She was soon off and skating with a smile that would have won an Olympic Gold medal. Johnny finished lacing his skates and went to bring Val her scarf, which she left on the dock. Underneath the scarf, JB found Val's Christmas present, a crappy old pair of strap-on boot skates. He covered them back up. Johnny skated with Val for a little while, all along as people came by and gave their hellos.

Someone shouted from up ice "Johnny, I'm gonna try my luck up stream. Might get some pickerel this time of year! Coming?" It was Wilton, Adas' dad, and he was looking for a fishing partner. Normally this time of year, people would ice fish, but Wilton was anxious to try out his new rod and reel, an expensive Christmas gift from his family. He would have to travel a little upstream to the open water. He was an avid angler and provided the family with fish all year long. Most of the islanders had a staple diet of fish from the plentiful Penobscot.

"Maybe later," Johnny shouted. "I still have to take care of business." Wilton waved and headed off.

No sooner did JB say that when the first negotiator came sliding by on his bottom 'jeckin', clipboard and pencils strewn about.

"Hey, Johnny! Have a pencil, compliments of Georgia Pacific. As you can see I'm not much of an athlete," said this proposition maker. "My name is Bert McCreavy and I"...SWOOSH-BOOM... and he fell, "...and I fall down a lot." He tried to stand and ... SWOOSH-BOOM... again, his legs go like rubber and down he went. " Can we talk over on the dock?"

"Sure, before we have to call one," Johnny punned, "What's your name again? " Niagra," he laughed. JB picked up a handful of pencils and helped Bert glide over to the dock and the two sat down for a lengthy discussion.

Meanwhile, Wilton was giving a few practice cast when he spotted something unusual across the river; a small dog was clinging to a floating log. The animal lover that he was, he ran a few yards to his dry- docked canoe and pushed it in the water, without hesitating to think of how treacherous the current and rapids could be this time of year. He managed to get across to the shivering dog and get it aboard, but had lost his paddle in doing so.

People were really enjoying the day. Ada peered out her window and could see Johnny sitting on the dock and now dealing with Jacko Breyhausser himself. She saw Mr. Breyhausser slip Johnny a small box of pencils. Still

another company associate, most likely Great Northern, nervously paced the nearby shore, waiting his turn to make an offer.

The perfect day was winding down when suddenly all eyes went upstream. Way up ice and just coming into view from around the bend was Wilton and he was in trouble. His canoe was barreling down the river, caught in the current and heading toward the solid ice. People started skating the distance toward Wiltons' drifting canoe to get in shouting range, but they were not going to make it. They screamed and yelled at him anyway, to at least sit down, waving their arms furiously. Wilton did not see nor hear their warning. He concentrated on the water movement. Johnny heard the commotion and skated to the vicinity but, he too, was late. With one loud crack, the canoe jumped up onto the ice and Wilton went over backwards, into the icy drink, one big splash and then nothing. The crowd gasped and went silent. They waited and hoped for Will to pop his head out of the frigid water, but too many precious seconds had gone by. Some ran down the shore toward the accident and others seized the runaway canoe with the dog still inside. Johnny was frozen in his tracks and glanced down to his skates and saw a horrible sight that he'd remember for the rest of his life. Under the ice, directly under him, there was Wilton, red coat and headband, scratching and clawing at the bottom of the ice, trying to find some air or breathing hole. The look on his face was one of shear panic and horror. The current had a hold of him and he moved so swiftly, they could only trace him for a few yards. Men with ice picks ran to the other end of the dam and started hacking away, hoping he'd still be conscious if the current took Will to their rescue hole. It was all in vain. The men got out the dragging equipment as Johnny tried to comfort hysterical Ada, standing on the ice in her housecoat and slippers. That night, about 8:30, through a big hole on the ice, Wilton Sockebasin came up on a hook.

CHAPTER 4

The following day was very somber. The whole island was in disbelief; shocked and saddened. Residents liked Wilton as much as they liked Johnny.

About 6:30 the next morning, Johnny was awoken to a distant repetitive sound. He opened the curtain and could only make out a figure down on the ice, chopping. It was Father Mulhaney, the local priest, and he was loading block ice onto a sled and hauling it uphill to a small hut behind the church. Normally, Johnny would be the first in line to offer a hand, but he knew today he would be busy. There would be a steady stream of relatives, friends, visitors and mourners and they would all have to be fed. Not to mention a church service at 10:00 A.M. in which Doe, as weak as she was, had insisted on attending.

Ada had a rough night and was sedated. Johnny had a spread of food fit for a king laid out by 9:30. He even cooked some of Wilton's frozen fish.

The small church on the reservation was packed to the brim. Father Mulhaney opened the service with, "The River giveth and the River taketh away". During the mass, a Great Northern representative had sat in the same pew as Johnny and slipped him a couple of pencils. Johnny looked over at him and the stranger motioned to go outside. If you have ever heard pencils snap in half in a quiet church hall, the sound is something like a firecracker. The Big Three was now down to two.

People came and went all day. Everyone was impressed with the display of food, even the fat Indian agent, Seymour Wiggins, though he would not eat any of the fish that Wilton had preserved.

"Superstitious," he said.

Later that evening, Johnny had informed Ada and her mom that he had signed a contract with Breyhausser and would be leaving in a couple of days. He sensed Adas' tears and went on to explain the contract. Along with his pay, Breyhausser gave him everything Doe suggested, plus a signing bonus, $300 in his name at the Penobscot Exchange, the freedom to hire not one, but two 'cookees', and he would only have to relocate camp once downstream when the log drive began. It was the only good news Doe had heard all day. He would meet the next morning at Marie's Chat & Chew and finalize the agreement over coffee.

Johnny walked the short distance to Marie's Chat & Chew and thoughts of the previous days events played back in his mind as he crossed the bridge. He could see the hole in the ice by the dam where Wiltons body came up, now frozen over. The bridge itself was a new modern convenience to the people living on the island. Before the bridge, the only way to the mainland was by canoe. Some even started a ferry business both for residents and tourist. In wintertime, some days would be plenty risky crossing the ice. It was still sad but not unusual to lose tribal members to the river. Wilton's death was the first since the bridge.

Johnny Boyle made his appointment on time and signed the contract with Breyhausser and upon returning to the island, he happen to walk by the Old Town Canoe Company. There inside, was one old employee, busily at work on some thawts...canoe seats.

"Mind if I look around," JB asked.

"Oh, you startled me. We're normally closed today but sure, help yourself," the old timer said. "I'm just tying up some lose ends here."

"Some fine looking canoes you have in here," replied JB. "It looks like a lot of work?"

"You got that right, mister. The price of lumber keeps going sky high. I don't know how much longer I can last," the boat builder pondered.

Johnny went to a corner of the lofty spaced warehouse and noticed a simple pair of skis, not too fancy, but efficient enough to get down a snow covered hill.

"How much for these?" holding up a ski.

The old man scrunched his nose and squinted through his glasses and chuckled.

"Those! You can have them skis. It's nothing. I made em' from scraps. Takes me a minute. I got a big pile of scraps. I could make a thousand pair with the pile I got out back."

Johnny had a brainstorm. "Listen...er...ah..."

"Bimpkin's my name, Sonny Bimpkins."

"Listen Mr. Bimpkins. Suppose I was to make a deal and guarantee you the best lumber at the best prices, and all it's gonna cost you is a little labor and a pile of scrap wood."

"Go on?" the old man looked very interested.

"I want everybody on that island to own a pair of these skis. Can you do it? Can it be done?" queried Johnny.

"Well, I think so. I sure have enough scraps of material, but how you gonna get this lumber?"

Johnny when on to explain all about his endeavors with the lumber industries and promised Bimpkins he'd have a fresh stock of the finest lumber by summer. They shook hands on the oral contract.

As JB was leaving, he passed a pawn shop. In the window was a pair of girls figure skates, white with silver laces, size 3, never worn, still in the box. He made this one last purchase before returning to Ada's. He gave the skates to Ada and instructed her to give them to Val as an early birthday gift. Ada smiled, for her heart was as big as Johnnys.

In early afternoon, Johnny was at my doorstep with an offer my family could not refuse. First off, I was to make a list of who I thought were the three strongest Injuns on the island, then came the offer to become his 'apprentice cookee' at $2 a day. I would have to miss the last half of the school year, but we surely

20

needed the money, and I would gain the knowledge that my little schoolhouse could never provide; hands on experience. My dad was all for it and had no problem giving Johnny permission. I was packing. We'd leave early in the morning.

CHAPTER 5

Johnny must have said his goodbyes the night before because he did not want to disturb Ada and her mom. The morning we left for Township #31 was exciting, fun and humorous. We had to hitch up Johnnys' trailer, which he kept behind Ada's house, to the pick-up truck to carry the three big Indians we chose to help haul 'Black Mac'. Johnny kept referring to them as 'the sumo wrestlers' and he had me laughing. The trailer was jury-rigged by a band of so called Penobscot mechanics, and made from the back of an old Ford pick-up and an old fish market cart. In fact, just about every motorized vehicle on the island was somehow jury-rigged. It was something they called Injun-uity.

The trip was long and bumpy, and we rested many times to let the wrestlers thaw out and change their blanket wraps. They had to take turns riding two on the trailer because we only had room for three in the cab. I offered to take my turn back there, but for whatever reason, Johnny wouldn't let me.

Our first stop was at the Penobscot Exchange in Bangor. In the 1930's, this was an important meeting and communication center, and most of our supplies would come through here. Johnny booked two rooms and spent some time setting up his account while the wrestlers and I got acquainted with the city. Johnny went shopping and bought some needed supplies and ordered us to get a good nights sleep because we would be loading the trailer in the morning. We'd arrive at Township #31 by noon the following day.

Load the trailer, we did. I became quite good at recognizing labels on the outside of crates. Johnny briefly showed me another holding chamber with crates marked <u>DANGER</u> <u>TNT</u> . He explained that the dynamite would be used during the log drive for blasting away stubborn log jams that the men could not free with ordinary tools. It would be picked up later, when the drive actually began. I asked Johnny what the skull and crossbones signified on crates marked for the paper mills and he responded that it was chemicals of some sort. Johnny backed up the truck at the warehouse exchange loading docks. There were many assorted boxes and crates, grouped on different pallets and headed for different locations. We found the three pallets marked TOWNSHIP #31 BREYHAUSSER.

We got busy and loaded crates and crates of produce, mixing dough, oil, butter, sugar, lard, salt, crackers, matches, pots, pans, soap, blankets...so much that Johnny had to secure three train tickets for the wrestlers to travel the rest of the way by rail. We had run out of room, even with the trailer. The plan was for Johnny and I to continue driving and unhitch the trailer at the camp. He would pick up our helpers at the train depot at Sherman Station, Maine, a one horse town but only 12 miles from Township #31. We dropped off the wrestlers at the depot in downtown Bangor so they could catch their train, and we started on our way. There was now barely any room in the cab for even me.

I was really impressed with how Johnny ran the show. He had a plan for everything. If someone threw a wrench into his program, somehow it was solved in a matter of seconds. Spur of the moment decisions. It was as if he had a back up plan for his back up plans. No mulling, just do it. When we arrived at the main camp, things went so smoothly. I was soon to see why Johnny Boyle was becoming such a legend.

CHAPTER 6

The very first thing I noticed when we arrived at the main camp was how noticeably cooler it was. There had been six inches of snow on the ground, compared to only a tracing back at the reservation. 'Old Betsy' did not get stuck once, and Johnny believed it was the good luck of 'Black Mac'. I think I believed that back then, but I now believe it was because of the weight of 'Black Mac'. A man was standing on the nearby lake, chopping and sawing ice into blocks and loading them onto sleds. He dropped what he was doing and came over to us. It was Moses Moore, surprisingly a young black fellow, 30 or so, and a little on the chunky side, or maybe it was all the animal hides he was wearing. Johnny introduced us.

"This is Moses Moore, we call him Moze," and I was told to pay strict attention to whatever he does. I could not help staring because it was the first time I had ever seen a black man, let alone have a conversation with one. My mother told me that we had a lot in common with their race as they too struggled with the U.S. government.

"Howdy ya'll, nice to meet yous'. JB, we'ze best get moving our humps cause we'ze fallen behind already," Moze pointed out with a slight southern accent.

"Right," Johnny agreed.

Moze was Johnny's 'cookee' from previous years and was very knowledgeable as to how JB operated out in the woods. I could see JB's breath as he spoke. A chill came over me and I gave a quick shiver. I was anxious to get started so I could generate some body heat.

We didn't waste any time unloading the goods onto sleds as Moze had informed us that the first team of horses would be arriving in the morning, followed by the men and tools. We had to hurry to get set up. We unhitched the trailer and Johnny sped off to Sherman Station train depot. He had to fetch the wrestlers, still hauling 'Black Mac'.

This gave me time to get acquainted with Moze and I quickly found out how he was Johnny's right hand man. You could tell that this man had done this routine many, many times before.

"C'mon! Bring yer stuff," he commanded. "This way."

He led me up a snow beaten path about 50 yards from where we left our supplies. I could smell smoke coming from the stack of the warming hut that we were headed for or it could have been from the huge bonfire that we passed. We passed a seating area consisting of the longest plank table I'd ever seen, with 4 benches. The warming hut, or dingle, was nothing more than a small square weather-beaten shack. I noticed it had a porch with new wooden steps.

Moze pointed to a corner door and motioned for me to inspect it.

"That's yers," he said.

It was a tiny room with one back window, just about the size of my bedroom back home. It had a fold down bunk, two blankets and an old pillow. A beaten fishing net nailed to the wall would hold my clothes. The room had a little wood stove which was already throwing heat. Moze must have set it for me as a welcoming gesture. It kept the room nice and toasty and I knew I would be cozy in my new bedroom.

"O.K.?" Moze asked, as I think he waited for my approval.

"Nice," I answered.

The main hall had a new floor and a five big tables and benches. On one wall, a big metal can connected to a stack was throwing heat. It was our wood stove incinerator. Moze pointed to it and grunted "trash". The other wall had a stone fireplace and mantle.

I could see another room in the opposite corner and figured it out to be Johnny's headquarters. Moze told me his sleeping quarters were in the hovel, or horse barn, a kind of fortified lean two.

He wasn't the type to chat much, only when he had something important to say.

"So, you've been with Johnny before, huh?" I tried to break the ice.

"Yep. Fifteen years now." End of conversation. I tried again.

"Do you play baseball? I do." He didn't answer.

Moze opened a huge back door and we walked down a plank to the ground. He pointed in the direction of over and down a hill somewhere.

"That's the outhouse." I could see a path leading over the hill but I figured I'd investigate it when I had to go.

Directly behind the shack was a huge tin box with a door and roof. The outside was draped with barb wire from the sawdust ground to the sheet metaled walls and ceiling, most likely to protect the contents from animals. Moze stood like a military general and began to bark out a list of instructions that must have lasted for a good five minutes.

"This is the tin kitchen. Over here is where the stove will go. Don't touch the stove when it's going. We keep the firewood here. Here's your work table and a bucket underneath. This is where you do the dishes, chop vegetables, peel potatoes, color the butter, fill jars, filet fish…, keep your supplies here. Keep things clean. Bean pot goes here."

Opening the door to the tin refrigerator he continued,

"This is where we hang the meat. Eggs go on this shelf, milk here, butter, lard, canned goods,…" and on and on and on. Everything had a place and I hoped I wouldn't forget.

Moze must have been in the process of lining the walls of the outdoor cold box with blocks of ice because the job looked only half done. This would be my first assignment. Moze instructed me how to layer each row of ice with a covering of sawdust. It was just as cold inside the walk-in ice box as it was outside, but I knew it would serve its purpose when the temperature climbed above freezing. He showed me how to saw and cut the ice blocks from the lake and using the tongs, we hauled them onto the sleds with bunk runners and up to the back of the hut. We worked until early evening and I started getting a little tired and hungry. Moze offered me some turkey jerky and it held me over, enough to help haul the rest of the supplies up to the outdoor kitchen. We unloaded them from the sleds, and started breaking open the crates, saving the wood for kindling. The 'Pilot Bread' cracker boxes were to be saved and used for boxed lunches only, for the times we had to take the meals to the men. Nothing got wasted. Somehow it became easier to remember where things went if you were the one who put it there. Moze and I loaded the shelves under his watchful eye. He was all business and I was beginning to like him and his work ethic. Where did Johnny ever find this guy? I could not even begin to speculate how a black man winded up in these parts.

Moze almost bragged to me that there were 29 men coming to this camp, the most they ever had to cook for. Six of the men were walk-on sign-ups when they learned Johnny Boyle was here. Two of them were well known lumberjacks and 'Babe and the Blue Ox' legends themselves. One came from as far away as the Yukon, and the other was from neighboring Nova Scotia. Another was an expert log driver and river man and switched over from Georgia Pacific after he, too, learned of Johnny being stationed here.

Johnny arrived with the wrestlers and the four of them had no trouble taking 'Black Mac' off the truck and getting it onto the tobaggans. Watching the wrestlers slip and slide on the snow as they pushed and pulled was too comical. Even Moze laughed.

Carefully, they set the stove in its place, and Johnny immediately started opening and closing vents and lids on 'ole Black Mac'. He tossed in some kindling and hay and started the seasons first fire. No sooner did the stove get hot when another truck pulled up at the site. It had 'Dahill Farms' written on the side and all of us went to meet it. The farmer greeted Johnny briefly and went to the back of his truck and swung open the homemade doors. I was amazed. There were whole sides of beef, lamb and pork hanging on hooks. It was an incredible picture to a kid of 12. He had cartons of chicken parts, eggs, butter, milk and sacks of potatoes...where did Johnny find this guy?

I thought to myself, "Not another load."

Needless to say, we were all busy the rest of the evening cutting, stocking, hanging, ...and finally... dinner. Wow!

'Black Mac' was aglow by now. Johnny spit on the hot griddle and I could see his spit bounce and roll right off.

"She's ready," he announced and grabbed his sharpest knife and disappeared into the cooler. Within minutes, he emerged and had six of the biggest cuts of steak one could imagine. With no seasoning, he tossed the steaks onto the stove and they smoked and sizzled immediately. He arranged the meat to one side of the griddle with one hand and, with his other hand, dumped a pool of oil on the other side. Moze had diced up a mound of potatoes and Johnny threw a portion of them into the now boiling oil and began to swirl them around. Moze chopped an onion and threw it in between the potatoes and steak and the aroma made my stomach gurgle. Johnny raked the onions over the steaks and through the potatoes and motioned for me to get six plates. In less than ten minutes, we were eating, all six of us. Johnny surprised us with six bottled Coca-Colas.

Now I don't know if it was the way Johnny prepared dinner that night or if I was just so hungry or if steak tastes better when its cooked camping out, but that was the biggest, tender, succulent piece of beef I had ever, ever eaten. Even the potatoes melted in your mouth as much as the steak did. I ate it all and felt so content, but we still had work to do. I had to boil kettles of snow and melt it down to water, both for drinking and doing dishes, before I could retire that night. Moze took the wrestlers to unload bails of hay in the hovel and to set up their sleeping quarters. They would sleep in sectioned off cubicles in the hovel and tend to the horses. Johnny cleaned the griddle and said goodnight, reminding me that we'd be up at 3 a.m. When I hit the sack, it was lights out. I took out my rabbit fur and placed it on my pillow. I liked the feel of the soft fur on my face. The men would be arriving soon and I thought it best that I get my rest now. I was going to need it.

CHAPTER 7

3 a.m. came sooner than I thought, even for this early riser. Johnny swung open the door to my room and with one spoon and a big fry pan, rang the alarm clock.

DING-DING-DING

"Good morning, Les. Rise and shine. Lets go."

Now I've heard a lot about hangovers and loud noises, but I never thought I'd experience it.

I sat on the edge of my bed and yawned and stretched. Before I could figure out where I was, my nose started working ahead of my eyes and the smell of bacon permeated my room.

I quickly remembered my scenario and got dressed in an exciting and anticipating moment. I entered the dining area and peered out back and JB had already had the stove fired up and breakfast ready. Johnny must have worked through the night because he had a mountain of biscuits prepared.

There were five plates set out on one table and Johnny informed me he had already eaten. He handed me a tray with a plate of food covered by a cloth napkin, along with a small pot of coffee.

"Take this to the bunkhouse... and hello Moze and the wrestlers," he commanded.

My first orders of the day and I was already confused.

"Bunkhouse?" I said with a puzzling look.

Johnny pointed in a direction and merely said,

"Jacko Breyhausser. He's here...in the bunkhouse" ...and so he continued knowing I was a bit confused...

"And hello Moze and the wrestlers. That means to tell them the <u>soups on</u>. You know... breakfast is being served. Got it?"

"Oh, Okay," and off I went.

I stepped out onto the porch with tray in hand and could only assume it was a hearty breakfast for the boss. I could see the bacon grease staining through the napkin. I peered over in the direction that Johnny had pointed to and was surprised to see a fairly large cabin with a light on. I did not even notice this the day before. Smoke was coming from the stack. A fresh blanket of snow had fallen overnight and the temperature was easily in the single digits. A light wind had whipped up and was biting at my face as I made my way to the bunkhouse and I came to appreciate my little wood stove in my room even more. I had no idea it was this cold outside. I had to get the food there in a hurry so it would not cool off but I also did not want to slip and fall and flub my first assignment, especially a delivery to the big gun. Mr. Breyhausser surely must have arrived sometime during the night. I took careful steps. As I approached the door, I started wondering how do I knock with both hands full. I was an ice skater and had pretty good balance so I thought I might balance on one foot and gently knock with my other... a perfect plan.

KNOCK ...KNOCK... KNOCK ...as I stood balancing.

"Come in," a voice commanded.

For what seemed like eternity, my mind went blank. I knocked with my foot again.

KNOCK KNOCK KNOCK...

"Come in," was the reply. Same thing, only louder.

"Oh, Great," I thought to my non-thinking self. I went to kick for a third time when my balance finally gave out and I started toppling to one side, just as the door swung open and the tray was snatched from my hand.

"Damn it! I said come in."

"Timber" and down I went, into the briar bush covered with snow.

Mr. Breyhausser placed the tray on the floor and stepped outside to offer me his hand. I shot up and brushed myself off. I had to think of another answer to a stupid question.

"Why didn't you holler something?" Jacko asked.

"DUH". Cause I only fwee years old and go to kindygarden," I said to myself. I didn't answer him.

"Come on in." Jacko said. He wanted to get a close-up look at the klutz. He picked up the tray and placed it on a table. The room was large and had enough bunks to sleep an army.

"I'm Mr. Jacko Breyhausser. I thought you might have been Vaughn Oliver, my foreman," he offered.

"No, just me…Les. I work with Johnny Boyle," I introduced myself.

"Well, Les, Johnny sure knows how to pick his helpers, so I'm sure you're gonna work out fine." He tore into his breakfast and I wasn't exactly sure how to take that last comment.

"I wish I had his talent for choosing the right men," Jacko marveled.

"Well, it was good to finally meet you, sir. I've heard only good things about you. I've got to get back now," and I turned to leave.

"Just a minute. How old are you, kid?" he questioned.

Uh oh…here it comes. He's going to tell me I'm too young to be here.

"I'm 14 and three quarters, almost fifteen," I answered proudly.

"Anytime you want to send a letter home, you bring it here. Anytime you get mail, you can pick it up here. Here's some pencils and paper." He reached into a night stand and handed me a fistful of pencils and a small stack of paper, with one envelop.

"It's good to write home, kid, so you don't get so lonesome. You know three months before the ice goes out is a long time."

"Well, I'll remember that sir. Thank you very much. Bye," and I closed the door. "Phew."

As I made my way to the hovel, I glanced down at the pencils Jacko Breyhausser had given me and saw his initials stamped on each pencil. The writing paper he gave me had Breyhausser etched into the bottom of the page. Why was he telling me to write home?

I reached the hovel and helloed Moze and the wrestlers that breakfast was ready. It was real warm in the hovel, maybe because of the hay and sawdust. The wrestlers were repairing boards and dropped what they were doing and practically knocked each other out dashing over to the wongon. I walked back with Moze.

"We'll be busy today, but once we get rolling, it'll be routine. How'd ya sleep?" Moze was genuinely caring.

"I slept like a bug in a rug," I answered.

"Good. Good." Moze replied. "This morning I'm gonna show you how to make donuts... Ten dozen."

"Ten dozen!" I shrieked. "That's, let see"...my arithmetic was not too good..."122 donuts. Wow"!

"Wait a picken' minute. You got two extra," Moze corrected.

"Ahhh...one for me and one for you," I quipped.

Moze chuckled, "C'mon, lets eat."

I had no sooner finished my 6th piece of slab bacon when we heard the neigh of horses.

CHAPTER 8

We all came out to see the first team of horses that arrived, six of them. The morning light was just about to break through and the steamy fog created by the animals breath and perspiration made the scene eerie. I had seen and been around horses before, but never quite like these. They were huge, strong animals with hooves the size of buckets. They were so hairy they scared me. Vaughn Oliver, the driver, was towing three sleds. This was the man Mr. Breyhausser was waiting for... his foreman. He was as scary looking as the horses. He was a big brute of a man, and a beard with icicles growing in it. He seemed as cold as the day. He gave out a low WHOA and promptly got off the sled, walked up to the third horse on the right side and gave him a swift kick into the shin. The horse buckled a bit, neighed and gave the meanest evil eye back to Oliver that I had ever seen an animal do.

"Get this beast out of my sight afore I cut em' up and smoke him into glue."

"Hey, Vaughn, take it easy," Johnny comforted.

"C'mon inside. I'll get you breakfast. You can tell me about your ride." Vaughn mumbled and complained as he went inside the dingle with JB. Johnny turned and motioned with his head looking right at Moze.

"Ok guys, lets get these harnesses off and bed these trotters," Moze ordered.

The wrestlers fumbled with the hitches as we each grabbed a horse. Of course, I got stuck with angry Man 'O' War. The horse probably couldn't wait to bite or kick the first person to come near him, after what Vaughn did to him. He had calmed down and actually enjoyed me undressing his harness. The wrestlers each had trouble controlling their horse, and even Moze ran into difficulty trying to stable. My horse turned out to be a gentle lamb. The other horses didn't seem to like him. I was first to the hovel, stall #1. I gave him some water, tedded some hay, filled a pail with oats, and honestly, the horse turned and winked at me. I learned his name was 'Pinch Me'. I thought that was ironic because that's what I named and christened my very first canoe. He became my friend.

We had six horses and eight stalls that were soon to be filled. We could hear some hootin' and hollerin' off in the distance. It was getting closer. It was the men, 30 of them, and they pulled into camp with the last team of horses and two more sleds, one loaded with baggage, the other with tools. What a bunch. This stand of thick timber would be reduced to a pasture in less than three months time.

CHAPTER 9

If the men arrived at camp on a ship, I would have easily mistaken them for a band of pirates. Vaughn Oliver came out of the dingle with bits of egg on his beard and instructed the loggers to grab their gear and head for the bunkhouse. He was already cracking the whip. Jacko was waiting at the door. One by one, they filed past us and into the bunkhouse as Moze clued me in as to who was who, the ones he knew of anyway. They were all different shapes and sizes.

The Yukon legend, Yens Rutter, was a Paul Bunyan look-alike; 45, big, strong, bearded and knitted cap. The Nova Scotia wood cutting champion, Pierre LeBlanc, mid 30's, was as skinny as a rail. Moze assured me not to be fooled by his thinness.

"Those skinny arms work as steady as gears turning a locomotives wheels, when it comes to sawing trees," he leaned over and softly fed my ear.

The Zimmerman brothers of Darmiscotta were the youngest; early 20's, inseparable and always worked as a team. The sled driver, simply known as Kringle, look just like, you guessed it, Santa Claus; white beard, red jacket, black boots, big belly and jolly. All he was missing was his reindeer. I knew there would be plenty of tales and folklores coming from their lips.

The men were given time to claim their bunks and unload their baggage before Jacko started his itinerary meeting. The wrestlers tended to the remaining horses as Moze and I headed back for the wongon. Johnny would need our help preparing the breakfast for this troop of hungry soldiers.

I could hear yipping and yapping and an occasional outburst of laughter coming from the bunkhouse. I wanted so much to be at that meeting but our place was with Johnny. We went up the new steps of the wongon and into the dining hall and Johnny was setting the tables with tin plates and cups for the crew. He said they'd be here in an hour. Moze and I went down the ramp and immediately started in on the donut making. We built a small campfire next to the tin kitchen, put a washtub on the flames, melted down a keg of lard, ripped open an 80 pound bag of flour, and rolled and molded 120 donuts. I was a mess. I had flour from head to toe but was actually having fun. When the oil got bubbling, we could fry 10 donuts at a time. Johnny used his own bag of flour and stirred up a batch of pancake mix, dropping in frozen blueberries that Ada and her mom had picked. In no time, he was grilling pancakes, bacon and sausage, and stacking it to the side. The aroma was delightful. Moze finished up the pile of donuts while I added the packets of food coloring to the oleo. I then put jars of syrup and molasses on the tables. With only 15 minutes left, Johnny asked me to mix him up seven dozen eggs. I found the biggest bowl we had. I started cracking eggs faster than the steady chop of a woodmen's ax. I stood next to 'Black Mac' and poured and stopped, poured and stopped, on JB's command. Between pours, he'd squeegee a little pool of bacon grease with his spatchela, swirl and flip the eggs till they became solid, and like a magician, divide them into precise equal proportions and set them aside. Thirty servings of scrambled eggs...done. He yanked open the hatch on the warming oven and pulled out two racks of heated biscuits. He tossed the leftover potatoes we had the night before and sizzled them on the griddle.

The doors flung open and in marched the men. They each grabbed a plate and cup, and in single file, came down the ramp and into the buffet line. Cholesterol was unheard of. Johnny loaded each plate, scrambled eggs, six bacon strips, six sausage links, six pancakes, and two biscuits. I poured coffee and Moze passed out donuts. When the men were all seated, the room became dead silent, except for the erratic rhythm of scratching forks on tin plates, as they wolfed down their feast. Johnny was a smiling god. He stood next to us on the ramp, beaming, as we watched the gorge, then leaned over to me.

"Les. See if you can fetch me a hammer and nail somewhere," JB whispered.

"Sure thing," and I went into my room. I pulled a hatchet out of my backpack and pulled a loose nail from the floorboards.

When I returned to Johnny, he was holding a sign. He took the hatchet and nail and went over to the mantle and right above it, he hung, on the wall, his sign which read: BREAKFAST 4:00 A.M., 1ST LUNCH 9:00A.M., 2cd LUNCH 2:00P.M., SUPPER 6:00 P.M., SIGNED JOHNNY BOYLE, MOSES MOORE, LESLIE RANCO, 1930. The crowd gave a rowdy round of applause and cheer and I think they broke into a chorus of <u>FOR HE'S A JOLLY GOOD FELLOW</u> or something like that. Johnny almost looked embarrassed. He winked at Moze and me.

We started to cleanup and prepare for 2cd lunch. I looked at the tray of donuts, gone.

Moze pointed to the oil kettle where 2 donuts where still frying. He looked at me and grinned, "122," and I knew what he meant.

CHAPTER 10

We were cleaning up and Mr. Vaughn came bursting through the door.

"Breakfast over. Listen here," he demanded. All eyes went on the foreman.

He unrolled a detailed map of the area and tacked it to the wall. I kept glancing at the map as I cleared plates and could see the area was divided into 13 lots. Moze did not like that. He shook his head and told me that 13 were a bad luck number. The map was detailed showing the river, dams, mills, lodges, hovels, booms, rolling piers, tool sheds, and another main camp 30 miles downstream where we would relocate when the drive began. As Vaughn pointed to the map, he teamed up the men and barked out orders.

"Today we concentrate on Lot 12. Hudson, Littlefield, you got the boom on the ice. Rutter, Ames, Blanche, Hendy...cutters. Leblanc, Mitchell, Stanhope, Hebert...saws. O'Donnell, Mealy... scaffers. Zimmermans, spruce only, for the paper mills. Hatt, Bacon, McBride, on the shore, the rolling pier. Kringle, Bean, teamsters." Each man had a job and off they went. They all seemed quite happy to be working and it reminded me of the seven dwarfs as they grabbed their tools from the sled and disappeared into the forest. I wanted to see them in action but I knew I would get a chance later. Besides, I had to use the outhouse.

My first trip over the hill to the outhouse was uneventful, other than finding a big cardboard box of toilet paper inside. The word <u>Breyhausser Paper</u> was stamped on the outside of the box. Toilet paper was pretty much a luxury item, and here, out in the middle of nowhere, was a case of it.

When I got back to the kitchen, I helped Moze dig a hole and prepare for cooking beans. He had soaked the beans overnight in the bean pot. We built a fire in the hole. When the embers got red hot, we threw in some big stones that would retain the heat. We worked as a team and manned two strong, sturdy poles, squeezed under the lip of the heavy bean pot, lifted and carefully maneuvered it into the hole. Moze threw in some salt pork, and I put the lid on it. I thought we were going to have beans for lunch but Moze told me they were for tomorrows lunch. It would take one whole day for the beans to cook. Later on, the wrestlers had even taught Johnny a few recipes of the Penobscots, birch root soup, fiddleheads and Oak Hill bread, just like home. Today's lunch would be boiled ham, potatoes, cabbage and carrots, a New England boiled dinner, served with biscuits, tea, and cookies. It was one of my favorites. Johnny was already fast at work.

The first two weeks of logging camp went by very fast and Moze was right; it became routine. The men worked till exhaustion. They were served four meals a day and the whole operation was working like a well-oiled machine. Each day, the ice slowly became dotted with massive logs. The January thaw came and went and the days were getting noticeably warmer.

Every other weekend, the men were given passes and most of them headed for the Penobscot Exchange in Bangor. Bangor was a bustling place of activity in its heyday. Flophouses, rooms with showers, speakeasies, hotels, restaurants, shops and street vendors all added to the flavor. The loggers would turn their paychecks in at the Penobscot Exchange in return for credit. Everything was put on tabs and when you were out of credit, you were out of money and headed back to the camp. Johnny would often go down with the wrestlers and stay overnight, but it was usually on business or to pick up supplies.

While no one was at the camp, Moze and I would ice fish. Twice a day we'd bust through the ice forming on our ice hole to keep it from freezing over. It was not only a good source to get fresh water and restock our water vessels but this fishing hole was magically productive when it came to actually catching fish. Our daily catch would impress Johnny so much that, on Friday nights, he would put on an all-you-can-eat fish fry.

After the fish fry, Moze would let me borrow his big washtub and heat up some water so we could take hot baths. He made a yellow soap from boiling down animal fat and adding a pinch of lye, similar to Fels-Naptha my mother would buy. It was good for bathing and washing clothes as well. He always let me go first and he used the same water after me.

It didn't occur to me then, but afterwards, I realized that somewhere in Moze mind it was bred that only a black man should share the water after another black man. It was as if he was not good enough to go first. One night, I had sniffles and was catching cold when Moze made me a poultice rubbed onto a flannel piece of cloth, and placed it on my chest. By morning, my symptoms had all but disappeared. I began to see how living in the woods can turn any skin color into red. I spent most nights with Moze and the wrestlers in the hovel, telling stories and playing cards and games. He had taught us the game of dominos from his hand carved set of over 1000. Before we actually ever learned it was a game, we spent many nights in the corner of the dining hall setting up sophisticated and elaborate trains and trails of dominos, sometimes spending days on it, only to watch them fall. It was just as much fun.

The wrestlers would amuse us with their stories of Penobscot lore. My favorite tales were that of Gluskabe, a figure of power and ingenuity, a hero and a trickster, who dealt with many of the forest animals. He was a fun spirit. It seems the wrestlers also feared a water monster they called Wiwiliamecq, a 40 foot long, snake-like, lizard like, sea serpent who fought shaman John Neptune in a watery battle that forever made the lake Nesiak, muddy and roiled. By far, their tales of Majahundu, the devil, frightened me the most. When something was not right or went terribly wrong, it was Majahundu. Even the name scared me.

Johnny would have many different friends and visitors in the course of a season. He really liked center stage and showing off his trait of what he did best... cook. He would always feed the men first, his guests second. Once in a while, an occasional hunter or trapper would pass through with rabbit or pheasant, and after some wheeling and dealing and consulting with Breyhausser, the fresh game would be on the weekly menu. It added variety.

Three months had passed and this camp had endured five major snowstorms, fourteen solid days of below zero weather, two lost fingers, a broken leg, two broken ribs, one case of pneumonia, one case of hypothermia, one strain of flu that knocked everyone off their feet for about a week, and two crushing injuries to some haul boys. It seems they got in the way of a runaway sled loaded with timber. Men would report to sick bay and, with Johnnys' homemade chicken soup, they'd be back on their feet sometimes in a matter of only hours.

The last two months had passed by much slower than the first. I was growing homesick and took up Mr. Breyhaussers advice and wrote a letter home. I never received an answer and I couldn't understand why. Surely my mother would write back.

CHAPTER 11

It was on a Friday night just before our little groups fish fry and JB was doing the frying. Moze, the wrestlers, and myself were sitting on the porch as the temperature reached an unseasonable 52 degrees, creating a dense fog. It was the end of March and we sensed the log drive would begin sooner than we expected. We couldn't help but notice how the new porch was now a perforated cork board caused by the loggers cock shoes, or shoes with spikes. We heard the horses coming and I could hear Kringle, "Whoa". He had arrived with three visitors. I could not make them out too clearly but it appeared as though one mans legs were in chains or handcuffs. They made their way into Jackos headquarters.

"Soups on", Johnny yelled to us.

We entered the dining hall and Johnny had a tray of trout fried to perfection.

"Dig in guys, I have more on the stove," Johnny declared.

"We've got visitors, Johnny," Moze added.

"Did you see who?" asked JB.

"We couldn't see too good through the fog, but it looked like one guy was in ropes," I added.

"Oh! Really?" Johnny was interested. "I have a hunch who it might be."

"Me too," Moze added sarcastically.

"Who? Who?" I wanted to know.

Johnny proceeded to explain.

"Well, it's like this, Les. Every logging season, you're bound to lose a few good men. It's too late in the season to train new ones, so the paper companies put in a request to the government for replacements. Sometimes they have a felon or thief who's doing time, but one who also knows the logging business. They'll give him a second chance. It cleans out their prisons, we get a worker."

"You mean a criminal"? I asked

JB continued, "Usually a guy who's on the mend... promises to do good. They must figure there ain't much trouble a guy can get in way out here."

Just then the door flung open and in walked Seymour Wiggins, the government agent guy from the reservation. He slammed the door, stepped on to the floor and down went our 3 day train of dominos.

"Evening, Johnny, Moses. Howdy," he nodded to the wrestlers and myself.

Moze eyes went cold. He took his plate of fish and went down the ramp. I knew immediately there was bad blood between them.

"I got you a live one this time. A smuggler from Canada. We didn't want to take any chances he might run, being so close to his country. Brought a guard and we had to cuff him. His name is Walls. Walter Walls. He should do alright." Wiggins assured. "He's signing in now and I bet he's pretty hungry. What'cha eatin?"

"Fish, but I can fix you something else." Johnny got up from the table.

"Where'd you get it"? Wiggins wanted to know.

"Moze and I caught it," I said proudly.

"Out here. You're getting to be quite the fishermen, Les. Just like your dad. Don't bother fixing something special, Johnny. I'll eat the fish if you've got enough."

"Yeah, OK, there's plenty. Get him a plate, Les... and bring a plate over to the guard and Walter... was that his name?" Johnny questioned as he sat back down.

51

"Yeah. That's right. Walter Walls, from Canada. I don't think he'll run. So how's Moses doing?" said Wiggins.

"Moze is good. How are things back at home?" JB inquired.

"Oh! That reminds me. I got a letter for you. Special delivery." Seymour dug inside his top coat pocket and handed Johnny an envelope. I knew Johnny received letters from Ada, but this one was of concern. It was from Doe, Ada's mom. He examined the envelope and noticed it had been suspiciously opened and resealed.

"Anything interesting in this letter, Wiggins?" Johnny accused.

Seymour choked, "Whatever are you saying."

JB gave him a dirty look and opened it slowly. He read it silently.

I went down the ramp to fix two plates of fish and noticed Moze was heating the water for our baths.

"What's the matter, Moze? Your face went as cold as a block of ice when Wiggins walked in. Do you know him somehow?"

Moze didn't answer, he just nodded. No one seemed to like this guy. Even the wrestlers cleaned up and offered to take the plates of food over to the new arrivals. They did not want to sit at the same table with Seymour Wiggins.

I helped Moze fill the washtub in my room. I took of my clothes and got ready to jump into the tub when Moze came in with the soap and towels. He sat on the bed with a tear in his eye.

"What is it, Moze?"

He sat silently, then he began to speak. He told me the startling tale of his broken family.

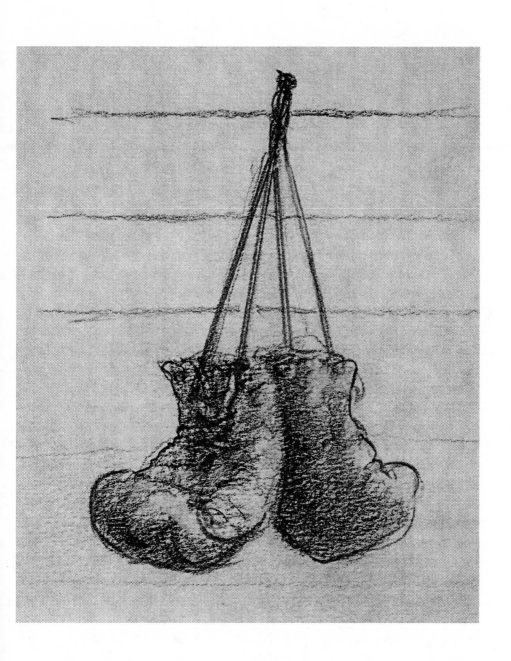

CHAPTER 12

Moze started to sob just a bit and tried not to show it.

"It was about fifteen years ago, and I was just a kid bout' your age. We was living in Boston, me and my mum and dad, just like Johnny Boyle. We weren't rich, but we wasn't poor neither. We had a little place, food... My pop was a prizefighter. He had many bouts, and with some of the meanest toughest men you'd ever laid eyes on. Each one went down, one by one. My dad refused to lose. His name was Samuel... Sammy... and they nicknamed him Slammy...that's right... Slammy Moore. He fought for his pride, not so much da money. As good as he was, he never gots the big news. He was a black man. He needed one more win to try for a national title. We traveled to Hartford, Connecticut for a match with an Irishman from Springfield, Massachusetts. His name was Fightin' Floyd Finnegan and he had never lost neither. Johnny Boyle was at that match. He could tell ya. He wasn't much older than me but he remembers that fight. My dad took one savage blow to the head in the first round and it got him bleeding from the ear. The ref went to stop the fight but the boo's from the crowd stopped him. He let them continue fightin' and my father, blurry vision and all, kept punching. Every time the ref went to stop the fight, the boo's got louder. My dad was swinging wildly at somethin' he couldn't see and somehow, some miracle from heaven, he landed an uppercut in round eight and Finnegan hit the tarp. He was out cold and Slammy Moore won by a knockout. He won the chance for the national title fight, but now was going blind. All he could sees was shadows. We came backs to Boston and everyone was telling him to give it up... boxing. He was supposed to face the Mexican boxing champ in New York City for da title. If he could win dis fight, it would be the one that would make him famous. But he couldn't see. There was no ways a fight would take place in New York. His agent had a pretty good idea at da time. They moved the fight from under the lights in New York to under the midday sun in Mexico... an outside arena. The noon sun wouldn't cast any shadows and my father could at least make out what he was swinging at. My mum and I, we didn't want him to go, but he was stubborn as a mule and had to prove something. We waited in Boston for word. It never came. The fight went on... and to this day...I still don't know what happened. My father disappeared off the face of this earth. The next thing I knew, my mum was being taken away by men in white suits and I was whisked up here in the woods. I ain't never heard from either one.. Old Wiggins out there, hooked me up with Johnny, and I've been going from camp to camp ever since. To think I've spent most of my life on these waters and I don't even know how to swim or hold my breath underwater."

"Wow!" his story was intense. "So what do you think happened?" I asked.

"I have a pretty good notion," Moze continued. "My father would not give up. If he traveled all the way to Mexico for a national title, he would not lose. I knew him. He'd rather die. I think, to this day, that somehow he won that fight down in Mexico and should have been crowned the champion." Moze continued in a disgusting tone.

"The U.S.A. was having its own problems with Mexico and rather than have their friendly neighboring country to the south be humiliated and disgraced and demoralized by, of all things, a black, blind boxer, the fight was what they called null and void and scrubbed off the record books. It was to be kept hush and I was told not to tell no one my dad was ever boxer, or maybe I'd never see him again. That's what I think happened, and someday... I will find the truth."

55

"What about Johnny? Doesn't he know?" I asked.

"I've sat and talked with Johnny about it, and even he has looked for the truth. We tried to get it out of Wiggins, but he honestly don't know nothing. He's just a puppet and only knows what the government tells him to do. I've been on my own ever since, fending for myself, wondering bout' my mom, teaching myself how to do things...to think I've been around this water most of my life now, and I don't even know how to swim or hold my breath underwater."

I was stunned. I didn't know what else to say.

That night, I did offer Moze the tub first and proceeded to teach him how to hold his breath underwater. It was something I could finally do for him. He forced a smile.

Just as Seymour Wiggins left a bad taste in everyones mouth, Johnny's letter from Doe that he delivered was equally depressing. After our baths, Moze and I came from my room and saw Johnny seated at one of the tables with the letter in his hands. Wiggins had left.

"Les, I need you to sit down," he seriously said. "I have to read you something I got from Adas mom." Johnny began reading as I sat across from him and Moze reset the fallen dominos.

He began: "Dear Johnny, I hope things are going well there. Things are not here. I am still weak but worried sick about Ada. She's been depressed ever since her fathers death and spends too much time taking care of me. Sometimes she mumbles sentences that make no sense to me at all. She is not eating well. She is pale and lacking vitamins. She complains of having no energy and is not herself most of the time. Maybe she needs a vacation. She feels good one day and bad the next. Same as me. Today is a good day for me. I feel fortunate as we have lost four elder members of the tribe already this year alone, due to sickness or flu's. Les' dad, Joe, is driving truck for the WPA and gone most of the day. His wife, Emma, was seen leaving one morning to go pick fiddleheads, in the middle of winter. You know as well as I that fiddleheads don't come out till May. She was seen leaving her house with only a sweater and a backpack strapped on. She was not found till 4 o'clock in the afternoon and came near to dying of exposure. She did have a little bout with pneumonia. Some say she's gone nuts. She is ok now, for the time being, but Joe may well have to quit his job to keep an eye on her. I know it's still two weeks away till the ice goes out, but it can't come soon enough. Hurry home, love Doe.

P.S. Do not let Ada know I wrote this.

P.P.S. Val loves her skates.

Johnny looked at me.

"Well, Les. I'll leave it up to you, but I think you might consider cutting your time short here and heading home. Sounds like you're needed."

"I guess I really don't have a choice. Do I?"

"I can arrange for Ada to meet us at the Exchange next week and she'll take you back, OK?" Johnny asked.

"Well...I guess. Maybe that explains why I never got a letter. She probably doesn't even know who I am? What's wrong with her?"

It was my turn to cry.

CHAPTER 13

I convinced Johnny to let me stay at least till the drive began and we relocated camp. I was here for three months and there was no way I wanted to bail out now. Not now, not at the start of the drive. To ease my guilty conscience, I wrote another letter home and assured my parents I loved them and would be home in about two weeks.

Spring had come early and the melting ice was too treacherous to walk out on now. The once solid lake had become a floating mass of pine, oak, spruce and maple. By now, all the men wore cock shoes and the already perforated entrance to the wongon began to look like shredded wheat. The spikes on their shoes enabled them to walk on the wet and slippery floating logs. The river men were incredible acrobats to watch, bouncing from log to log, and having fun at it. Pick poles and cantdogs were now everyday tools, aiding the loggers in positioning and moving key logs. It reminded me of a gigantic pick-up sticks game as they rolled logs off of each other so each was floating individually.

The efficiency of the men and the great stand of timber were turning Township #31 into a very fruitful acquisition for Breyhausser. Even Jacko himself had on a pair of Bass cock shoes and was out rolling logs and inspecting the beginning of the river drive. It was very dangerous work. The slightest slip into the icy waters and down in between the logs you'd fall. It would mean death, if you could not find a space to come up for air, not to mention getting possibly crushed. Oliver Vaughn was extremely cautious and careful when hollering out the orders.

He was a good river man and was proving it.

Two bateaus, or logging boats were paddled up the river to camp, and the go ahead to release the boom was given. The bateaus were specifically designed for logging; slim and pointed, stable enough to stand steady and paddle, able to carry five men or more if need be, rode the rapids well, and were easy enough to maneuver to pick up any stranded loggers in tight situations.

The boom was a chain of logs laid across the lake like a floating dam, to corral the floating trees. Once it was reeled aside, the logs would start to flow with the current. The boom could be carried down river and used again, but usually some men were sent ahead to build another at some critical point when they wanted the drive to stop. Otherwise, sixty miles would be too long a ways to go without a break. It would scatter the men too sparsely. It had to be controlled.

As it was, the men had already been scattered enough. We had to pack their lunches in Pilot cracker boxes and take their meals to them. Kringle was our chauffeur, using one horse and one small sled. We were all busy.

A case of dynamite was brought in with one of the bateaus, and would be used only in a jam or wing where the key log could not be pole picked free. The rolling pier was now working overtime, as were the teamsters and their horses, hauling load after load of cut timber from the deeper parts of the forest. One by one, the logs were loaded onto the pier and rolled into the river, creating big splashes.

Once the mass of timber started moving as one, the cock shoed men walked out with their pick poles as if they were walking on land, carefully keeping an eye on any stray logs. One bad angled log could tangle and jam the flow, causing massive headaches and a days work for twenty men to try and free it.

With this many logs, I knew it would be impossible to keep wings from forming. There would be plenty of jams. The faster you could get to a jam, the easier it would be to bust the key log free. Men were running up and down the river, between landings.

There was an anticipating excitement in the atmosphere, sort of like when my baseball team was one inning away from nailing down the state title.

That drive began on the East Bank River, and eventually wound up on the great Penobscot River, the very same river that surrounded my reservation. It would pass through the town of Millinocket. Most of the wood was milled and bound for Machias Bay, where it would be loaded onto schooners and taken to New York by way of the great Atlantic. There, it would be distributed internationally. The smaller spruce logs would be weeded out and floated to the paper mills. We were feeling proud and quite international knowing we were a part of this whole successful operation.

CHAPTER 14

We left out a spread of cold food for the upcoming day and night for the men staying behind. Johnny and Moze would be back in the morning, I would be on my way home. Johnny, Moze, the wrestlers and myself loaded a sled with leftover food and supplies. Kringle would take us to the new location, the Main River Camp, 30 miles downstream. We passed out hearty lunches along the way. The sleigh ride down was one of the most majestic, scenic and peaceful journeys I had ever been on. None of us said a word, we just watched. Maine is so tranquil. There were still traces of snow on the ground, especially on the hard packed trail we were following. More mother earth was showing now than snow. Every once in a while... light, silvery snow brushed off the pine boughs as if some fairy was sprinkling her dust in the sunlight. The newborn animals were aplenty. Deer, moose, raccoons, chipmunks... all were playing and greeting spring. Birds were back and singing. Katahdin, the sacred Indian mountain, was in the background for much of the trip. The many clear, babbling brooks offered serenity to the ears. Salmon was in the river and a few black bears and cubs were seen fishing.

As Kringle and the now- not- so- hairy horses pranced us through the woods and over two- tracked paths, we came upon a bit of civilization. I could hear school bells, and the sound of machinery. The fresh pine scent in the air disappeared and it was replaced with a foul dump smell. I looked at the wrestlers but they were looking back at me as if I was the guilty party. I remember we pointed fingers at each other and laughed. We passed about a dozen houses scattered in a clearing and about 200 yards after them, still along the river, was a massive brick building with chimney stacks and water wheels. There was the big letter B on one of the stacks. It stood for Breyhausser. It was one of their paper mills. Johnny asked Kringle to stop and we got out to scout around. We crossed a rickety bridge near a dam, got to the other side, and we were greeted by a miller heading into the building.

"Can I help you guys?" he said suspiciously.

"We thought we'd look around at the operation. My name's Johnny Boyle and we work for Breyhausser."

"Johnny Boyle! So you're Johnny Boyle? Hmmm...I pictured you much bigger. Anyway...c'mon in. I'll be glad to show you round. The name is Foss, Milton Foss," and he proudly lead us into the building.

He had heard of Johnny and we got a grand tour, all of us.

It was so loud inside I could barely hear Mr. Foss speak, but he took us from station to station and explained each process of turning wood and pulp into paper. We passed a number of palettes with boxes of chemicals stacked six foot high. Foss spoke in numbers... the number of reams, the number of cardboard boxes, the number of machines, the number of employees, and on and on.

We thanked him for his patience and headed back across the shaky bridge to the other side. We hopped onto the sled and Kringle gave the mush signal. We traveled only a few hundred yards and out of sight from the mill and Johnny asked Kringle to pull over. Johnny went off the path and down to the river bank. We thought he had to relieve himself and waited patiently, but he was down there for a long time. His voice came through the pines.

"Les!...Les!... Bring me an empty box!"

"Okay, Johnny, right away," and I scurried to find an empty box. There was none, so I gave Kringle and the wrestlers their ham sandwiches early and took the cracker box down to Johnny.

I fought my way through the thicket and came to a high river bank. Johnny was down below, on the shore, almost standing in the river. I could not believe my eyes. Dead fish of all kinds were strewn about on the shore. It smelled rotten. The once crystal clear blue water was now the color of coffee. Dead muskrats, one beaver and a small fawn were laying dead in the muck. Crows were picking at the carcasses, next to, of all things, dead crows. I stood in bewilderment and wispered aloud, "Majahundu". Johnny motioned for the empty box.

"Bring it here." I made my way down to the riverbank.

"What is it, Johnny? What happened"? I wasn't sure.

"I don't know, Les. Grab me a stick."

I fumbled for a stick and passed it to him. He carefully tried to flip one fish into the box but it fell apart, loaded with maggots.

"I need another stick," JB asked.

I fetched him another stick and this time he balanced a fish and laid it in the box. He put the lid on it and made a pact with me.

"Listen, Les. Don't tell anybody about what we've found here until we can find out what it is."

"Well, Ok, Johnny but"...he interrupted.

"I have a friend at the Exchange who's like this scientist. OK? His name is Doc Meyers. He can tell us why this fish died. Okay? So don't say a word until were sure."

"Alright, I promise," and we turned to go back up the river bank and Moze was standing there watching us.

Moze didn't say a word but Johnny made him swear to the same agreement he gave me.

"Moze, not a word about this to anybody," he commanded.

We got back onto the sleigh and Kringle and the wrestlers were so busy munching their food they had not even questioned the box or what we had been doing. We rode on. The Main River Camp was 10 miles away and I would be going home soon.

CHAPTER 15

About another five miles down the trail, Johnny had to make one more stop at the Breyhausser saw mill. This mill was just as big as the paper mill a little upstream. He placed an order of wood for a man named Bimpkins. This mill would literally be buzzing in a few weeks time, especially with the load of lumber that we knew was headed down the river and soon to be at their conveyor belts. Once again, we were given a quick tour and demonstration of the powerful saws and machinery. Tree trunks turned into planks in a matter of seconds. Lathes that turned wood into bolts, shingles by the thousands. The biggest and sharpest blades and saws one could imagine. This was a factory in its prime, and orders were being sent out all over the nation. We said our thank you and continued on our journey to the relocation camp. Another hour and we reached our destination.

The Main River Camp was only two lodges and a series of campsites and campfires. It looked more like where the Boy Scouts would hold a jamboree. Unlike the first camp, the men would be moving with the drive so no one stayed here for any real length of time. Once again we set up a kitchen, started a bean pot, and cooked on an open fire. We did not need 'Black Mac' for the time being and for the few men we had in camp, but Johnny, the pick-up truck and the wrestlers would haul it down on the next trip. Of course, Johnny could cook on an open fire as well as with his stove. We served supper to the few loggers in camp that night and sat around the fire most of the night. We were closer now to the Penobscot Exchange and I would be leaving in the morning, with Johnny and Kringle, and we were to meet Ada.

The morning came and it was awfully hard saying goodbye, especially to Moze. He assured me we'd see each other again.

"Once a river man, always a river man. It gets in your blood," he used to tell me.

Johnny had the arrangements all laid out. We arrived in Bangor at noon. We went through the Exchange, got a hotel suite, train tickets for the next day back to Old Town, and reservations at Bangor's finest restaurant. We met Ada in the lobby at the Exchange.

"Yoo hoo! Hey, guys. I'm over here." Ada was seated on a sofa in the lobby, reading magazines.

"Look at you guys... mud and all. Was it a long trip?" she remarked.

"Pretty long," I answered.

"You guys look like you could use a hot shower? Anyway, hey Les, the guys on your baseball team...they were asking about you. They'll be glad to know your coming back." She always tried to make things easier.

"Johnny, look at your whiskers. You need a shave."

"Hi, doll. I told you I would grow a beard and never shave if I couldn't see you again," Johnny remarked. It must have been some private joke they had between them. We went the few steps across the street to our magnificent hotel and unloaded our bags.

I could sense that Johnny and Ada wanted to be alone so once again I took a walk through the city. Being in the woods for so long without seeing any women was even playing tricks on my hormones. The hookers were obvious, appealing to the men who had money. One approached me and my knees started shaking. I quickly shied away, running all the way back to the Exchange. About three hours had passes and I unexpectantly dropped in on Johnny and Kringle, who were having a mild discussion in the Exchange lobby.

"Please, JB, please. I thought I had more credit than I do," Kringle said drunk. Somehow, somewhere, in a matter of only hours, Kringle had gotten stone drunk.

"Just this once, JB...please. I dropped off that stinkin' box like you told me too...to that Doc Meyers! He's out of town, I tell ya!" Kringle was slurring his words.

"Alright", alright," JB said as he turned to the desk clerk.

"Let him have a room, one dinner, one breakfast, and no alcohol. Make sure he has a wake up call at 6:00 a.m."

"Oh, c'mon Johnny." One nightcap, just one" Kringle pleaded.

"Your tab, Johnny," the desk clerk responded.

"Yeah, but no alcohol." Johnny was adamant.

He looked once more at Kringle.

"Take it or leave it."

Kringle stormed out mumbling to himself. Johnny yelled to him.

"We'll be going back at 8:00 in the morning so get a good nights sleep."

Johnny was chuckling a bit as he watched Kringle stagger out, and turned to me.

"Don't ever start drinking, kid. Hey! Aren't you ready yet? C'mon! Back to the hotel and get dressed! Adas waiting and someone's cooking dinner for us for a change."

We went to our beautiful hotel room and I could take an actual hot shower. I put on my cleanest dirty shirt, spruced up my hair, and was ready to go.

Ada looked fine to me. Not a sign that there was the slightest thing wrong.

"Has he been taking good care of you, Les." she asked.

"The best, for being out in the woods," I replied.

"That's good to hear. He does know how to take care of people he likes," she remarked looking sexily at JB.

Ada looked stunning with a long white gown, and a fox stole. I saw her put on make-up, but she wore it in a way you couldn't tell she was wearing any at all.

Ada and Johnny walked arm and arm to the classy restaurant, and I followed behind. I was stunned to see three different hoboes and beggars recognize Johnny and ask for a handout. They called him by his name. He didn't give them silver. He gave them green. I don't know exactly how much, but I do know a dollar in those days went a long way. Everyone greeted Johnny and Ada as if they were from Hollywood. They did make a good couple.

The food was French and I didn't know what I was eating half the time. Some things tasted okay, especially the little chicken legs, which I later found out were frog legs. Johnny and Ada laughed at that one. The desert topped it off... a scrumptious fudge cake. The waiter smiled at whatever the tip was that JB left. It was all done on paper and through the Exchange. By now the word must of gotten around Tin Pan Alley because by the time we left the restaurant, a string of transients and lined the street. Again, Johnny gave them each cash.

Johnny and Ada headed off for a show and told me they wouldn't be out too long. I slowly made my way back to the hotel room still taking in the sights and doing some window shopping. Johnnie had given me a dollar, and I made the most of it at the penny candy store. I bought three bags, and strangely enough, it wasn't all for me. I found myself dreaming of getting back home and having Val and her friends greeting me. I would hand out the candy. Johnny was rubbing off on me.

I did eat a lot of the chocolate that night and my tummy was upset. Of course, I blamed it on the frog legs. When I made it back to the hotel room I was now exhausted and ready to sleep. A yellow telegram was tacked to our hotel door.

"Uh, oh,"...I thought. I didn't dare read it till Johnny and Ada got back. I laid in bed and moaned, and could not help but think of what sort of news, good or bad, was in the telegram. Was it about my mother? Should I have gone home two weeks earlier? I could not sleep, but I pretended to, as I heard the Hollywood couple come down the hall.

CHAPTER 16

They were laughing and giggling when they enter the room and I hated to ruin their night. I knew they would spot the telegram. They couldn't miss it. I placed it in a strategic spot on the coffee table. What was taking them so long to find it. I had to get up. I couldn't wait no longer. I came out of my bedroom and the two were embraced.

"Oh, Les, sorry, did we wake you?" Ada implied.

"What's the matter? Couldn't sleep in the big city?" Johnny added.

I pointed to the telegram on the coffee table. I picked it up and handed it to Johnny.

"This came. It was tacked to the door," I nervously stated.

"A telegram! What's it say?" Johnny asked while taking the letter.

"I don't know. I didn't read it. I was too scared to open it." I think I had a tear in my eye because Ada gave me her hanker chief and put her arm around me.

Johnny sliced through the telegram with a letter opener he found in the desk.

He silently read, then gulped, and slowly turned his eyes upon Ada and I, who were now seated on the couch. His eyes then stopped at Ada and he spoke.

"It's your mom, hon. She passed during the night."

"WHAT!" Ada screamed. "WHAT! It can't be!" She jumped from the couch and ripped the telegram from Johnnys hands.

: Dear Ada, STOP:

: Please return home as soon as possible STOP:

: Your dearest mother Dorothy has passed. STOP:

:Rested comfortable but did not make it through the night. STOP:

:My sympathy, Father Mulhaney. STOP:

Ada could not hold it in and burst into tears. She ran and flopped onto the bed. Johnny went in to comfort her as much as possible.

"I knew I shouldn't have left her. I knew it, I knew it," she cried, and she kept repeating that all night. Somehow, I got the feeling she was blaming Johnny. I was saddened by Does death, but I was more relieved it wasn't my mother.

It was a long, rough, night but we finally got a few hours sleep. Johnny had to buy another train ticket and would come back to Old Town with us. He asked me to keep an eye on Ada as he went to the Exchange. She looked a mess. I guess she did have on make-up because it was now running all over her face and eyes. She must have been crying all night, but somehow found the courage to be brave. Johnny had written a lengthy note to Mr. Breyhausser and had to find Kringle to deliver it. He had some instructions for Kringle to meet him at Sherman Station in three days. He also jotted down some quick notes for Kringle to deliver to Moze and the wrestlers, saying he would meet them back at Township #31. Moze was experienced enough to handle the cooking for a little while, and for now, 'Black Mac' would stay put till Johnny got back.

The weather was playing tricks on us. The mercury had dipped into the single digits overnight and it didn't budge much through the day. The ice was beginning to refreeze. This would create much havoc and danger on the log drive, possibly suspending it if the sudden cold snap didn't break.

Father Mulhaney picked us up at the Old Town station and drove us back to the reservation. I remember the feeling as we crossed the bridge. It seemed I was away for ten years and it felt so good to be home. Val was the first we passed and she happily waived as she and her friends were skiing down a small hill on what little snow was left. It was a little odd because, in just about every yard, I could see there were a pair of skis. We pulled into Adas driveway. It was dusk and Ada already had a houseful of people, and a pile of skis stuck in snow banks outside her entrance. Johnny brought Ada into the house and relatives and friends took over her care. Johnny himself was looking like he could use a good nights rest. He went to bed early, for another table of food would have to be put out the next day. The service for Doe would be at 9:00 a.m.

I darted the short distance home and entered our little domain. My mother was knitting, and my father was sharpening his ax.

"Hey, mama, look who's here?" my dad said.

"Leslie, dear, come here, let me look at you. Oh, it's so good to have you back home. Look at you. You've grown. By and by, you'll be as big as your father. I made a pie," and my mother gave me a huge hug with her dirty apron on.

"We've missed you so much," as she squeezed. As I pulled my arms away, I snagged an envelope from her apron. It fell to the floor and I picked it back up. It was addressed to me and dated months ago. She had written, just forgot to mail it.

"Mom. Is this yours?" She looked dumbfounded at it.

"C'mon Les, lets have some pie and tell us all about your journey." My dad changed the subject.

I sat and talked for one solid hour and told them everything. Everything, accept for the dead fish incident which I had a pact with JB. They filled me in on what was happening around the reservation. They were both happy to see me and it felt so good to be home. I got into my bed that night, thinking about Moze and the wrestlers, and I thought of how cold it had gotten outside. The next morning, I heard a faint chipping noise, and went to my window. It was Father Mulhaney, down on the ice, and cutting blocks and loading them onto sleds. I got dressed in a hurry and ran down to the ice and asked if I could help. I was now experienced, and looking for work.

"Bless you for helping, son," Father Mulhaney sighed. "I've been looking for someone to do this job. I'm afraid I am getting a bit too old to handle this anymore. Are you interested? I can't pay as much as Johnny!"

"Sure thing," I responded.

"Its just till the ice goes out," the priest offered. "Next year you can do it all winter."

"It's a deal," and I loaded the block of ice onto the sled.

" Where do you want this, anyway"?

"Up behind the church. Follow me," and the priest led the way as I hauled.

He pointed to a little shack behind the church and simply stated, "In there", and pointed.

I held the door open with one foot and pulled the sled of ice into the shack backwards. I noticed shelves of ice lined with sawdust and it immediately reminded me of the 'tin kitchen'.

"You know, Father, up in the woods, at the camp, we had this outdoor kitchen that"... I stopped in the middle of my sentence as I rotated my head. I turned as white as a ghost. There, lying on the ice block shelves, were the dead bodies of Doe...and Wilton... and others.

I held my breath and ran to the outside of the door. I didn't throw up, but I came close. Father Mulhaney came out and tried to explain.

"They have to be preserved, son. We have to wait till the ground thaws in the spring before we can dig in the cemetery and give them a proper burial. Do you understand?"

I shook my head. I looked over at him and he almost was chuckling. Oh, I took the job, alright, but I only hauled as far as the door.

It was still brutally cold outside but Does service was warming. Ada was brave and Johnny stayed by her side. A gathering took place at Adas that afternoon and once again Johnny was the king of cuisine. He prepared what food he could, and again cooked some of Wiltons frozen fish. Neighbors brought a casserole, Oak Hill bread, venison, fiddleheads, and my mother baked another pie. There was so much food, Johnny had to light the warming oven on the stove. People came and went all day, but it was so peculiar to see Ada greet the same guests over and over. Four times she thanked me for coming, each time as if she had just seen me for the first time. I thought she was probably still a little in shock. I knew something was really wrong when I witnessed her feed the cat for the ninth time in two hours. This was really bothering Johnny. He had a discussion in the back room with the doctor scientist friend of theirs, Doc Meyers. They were both worried about Adas behavior, and rightly so. When Johnny emerged from that little meeting, he had a look on his face of anger. One I had never seen before.

Seymour Wiggins made an appearance and was probably there for the food only. A shouting match between him and Johnny surfaced.

"Loaded your plate up pretty good there, Seymour," Johnny asked.

" Johnny, you know your cooking can't be beat," he replied.

"I don't see any fish on your plate," Johnny inquired.

"I just haven't got room for it. I'm not much of a fish eater. Looks good though," Wiggins answered.

"Try the fish. Go ahead. Try it!" Johnny was insistent.

" No, I really, really...I'm really not too hungry...," Wiggins stuttered.

"Eat it", Johnny demanded and with that he picked up a piece of fish and tried to shove it in Wiggins mouth. Wiggins closed his mouth tight, dropped his plate and ran out. Johnny followed him to the door, yelling all the way.

"You bastard! You knew all along. You stinkin' fat bastard! Get outta town...you...you"... He was really upset. It was the only time any of us have ever heard Johnny raise his voice.

Wiggins left, calling everyone crazy and claiming he didn't know anything. One by one, people gave their condolences and left. Johnny had made arrangements with Doc Meyers for Ada to be taken to Boston to see a specialist. He would pay for it all. He knew he had to get back to work quickly or jeopardize losing his contract with Breyhausser. He would try and get a good nights rest and head back in the morning.

CHAPTER 17

Doc Meyers swore he would personally look after Ada and take her to Boston. He gave Johnny a lift back to the Exchange, said their goodbyes, and from there, JB caught a train to Sherman Station. He met Kringle at the depot and he was driving Johnny's truck.

"Hi, Kringle. What happened to the sled?"

"Oooh, Johnny. Breyhausser is mad, mad, and mad. He wouldn't allow me to take a team to fetch ya. I had to sneak away. The drive is frozen, with this screwy weather. Most of the men came back to camp and Moze is doing the best he can to feed them. I've been trying to help him. We gotta get back in a hurry," Kringle insisted.

"Well, let's go," and they hopped in the truck and took off.

"I'm sorry what happened, I mean, with your girls family and all," Kringle offered apologetically as they rumbled in the truck.

"Thanks, Kringle," JB Replied solemnly, and nothing more was said.

The two arrived in camp and noticed Moze out on the logs fishing. The reformed ice was treacherously thin.

"Look at him out there," JB pointed out to Kringle. "He's out there trying to catch enough fish for the entire crew, just to make people happy again." They watched for a minute and Moze turned and waved. With no cock shoes on, the slippery log he was standing on suddenly rolled. Moze did his best to gain his balance, but could not. With a crashing splash, he went through ,down, under and between the ice and logs.

Immediately, flashes of Wilton under the ice flashed through JBs mind. He exited the truck and ran towards the hole screaming at the top of his lungs.

" Moze. Moze...not Moze..." Johnny had certainly seen enough death in the last few months and was near panic when Moze fell through. Without even thinking, like a jackrabbit he bounced and hurdled over twenty logs to get to Moze. He laid his body across two logs and stuck his entire arm in the icy water. Kringle and Vaughn came running after, though not nearly as fast as JB went. He felt around for what seemed like eternity. After several minutes, to everyones amazement, Johnny had pulled Moze up out of the frigid water by the collar of his jacket. The men on shore cheered. He was unconscious and Vaughn carried him quickly to the shore. By now the wrestlers had heard the commotion and came running from the hovel. Without hesitation, one of them jumped on Moze chest and started pumping and the other gave mouth to mouth. After several tries, Moze came through and spit up some water. The other wrestler ran to Johnny and helped him to his feet. Jacko Breyhausser had come out of the bunkhouse and, after watching for a few minutes, ordered everybody back to work.

"I am trying to run a paper company. Everybody back to work... NOW...or there's gonna be some consequences...and Johnny, I want to see you in the bunkhouse."

Johnny, with arm still soaking wet, came over and knelt next to Moze and tried to hold up his head. Johnny could not feel his hand and used the other one to hold up Moze' head. Moze spoke softly.

"If you see the kid, tell him I held my breath," and he passed out again.

"Moze...Moze," Johnny shouted and shook. Oliver Vaughn picked up Moze and placed him in Johnnys truck. Kringle got in to drive and yelled.

" Let's go. He's got to get to Millinocket, and fast. The closest hospital was two hours away. No one knew if Moze would make it. They had to try and not waste any more time. The wrestlers came down with blankets and a poultice and made Moze as snug and warm as they could for the trip.

"Vaughn, Kringle! Jacko shouted as they drove away. No one paid attention to him. He disgustingly stormed backed into the bunkhouse and slammed the door.

Johnny could not feel his hand. The wrestlers took him to the wongon. One heated water in a fry pan on 'Black Mac', the other stoked the barrel stove and still one more sat him by the fireplace, took off his wet jacket, and threw it on Les' old bed, in exchange for the blankets in the room. An envelope had fallen out of the wet jackets pocket and stuck in between the bed and wall. The wrestler did not notice.

They wrapped Johnny in the blankets. He put his hand in the warm water, and still could get no feeling. He got up from his chair, wiggled his fingers, walked down the ramp, and put his hand over 'Black Mac'. He stood there for a few seconds and still could feel nothing. What happened next and for whatever reason, he then placed his frozen hand onto the griddle of the glowing stove, and it seared for the brief second he had it on there. He raised his hand to look at it, and still felt nothing. He had a scared look on his face. The wrestlers put a salve on his injured hand, and proceeded to cook lunch, under Johnnys direction. He wasn't himself and retired to his room.

Later that night, as cold as it was, he had to know how Moze was doing, and hitched up a sled to Pinch Me. As if Pinch Me knew the urgency of his dire mission, he rode through the night to Millinocket Hospital, like a horse vying to win the Triple Crown. By now, Johnnys unprotected hand had turned a waxy, white as he tried to hold onto the reigns. The temperature was below zero. He was he immediately looked at upon arriving at the hospital, but he refused treatment and wanted to see Moze. Vaughn and Kringle were vigilantly seated in the lobby, awaiting word, when Johnny entered the waiting room.

The news was not good. Moze had suffered some sort of brain damage. Johnny wanted to pay for his treatment, and to see that he rested well. The doctors assured him that Moze was in the best of care and convinced Johnny to see a specialist in Boston. He only agreed when the doctor mentioned Boston, perhaps cause he thought of seeing Ada. Kringle would drive him in Johnny's pick-up. Vaughn took the horse and sled back to the camp, and brought the disheartening news.

CHAPTER 18

The rest of that year, I kept a close eye on my mother. My father gave her steady doses of spring tonic, or sulfur and molasses, and it must have worked because even as Ada deteriorated, my mother gradually improved. He was able to keep his job at the WPA. She never recalled the fiddlehead incident, but she did remember my birthday and asked what I wanted.

I wanted to visit the camp, township #31. We took my dads new truck, new to him anyway, and made the journey. The camp was as empty as a broken hourglass. I walked around as my mother and father gave me some time to reflect. I went onto the porch and looked down at the shredded wheat pine boards. I went into the wongon and it smelled a bit damp. The lunch sign was hanging crooked and I took it off the wall. My old room was exactly the same as when I first plunked down my baggage. I sat on the bed and stretched, then laid down. I could hear the horses neighing. I wondered who Pinch Me was giving a hard time to now. I wondered if Wiggins had gotten some criminals to replace Moze and I, and even Johnny.

As I almost drifted off to sleep, my arm fell in the space between the wall and bed, and I felt a piece of a paper. I reached down further to grab it and came up with my old rabbit skin. I felt again for the paper and it had fallen further. I had to climb off the bed and physically move it aside. Under the bed, I found some dominos, and some pencils with the initials J.B. on them.

I finally got the letter, sat on the bed, and opened it. It was a letter from Doc Meyers:

Dear Johnny,
    The tests were complete and the results are positive. The fish was contaminated with   mercury. The mercury poisoning is, without a doubt, what caused the death. Mercury is a chemical that is highly toxic to fish and animals as well as humans.
    If you need to know more, contact me at my house in Bangor.

signed Doc Meyers

Now I find it strange that Doc Meyers was murdered over the summer. They say it was an intruder that Meyers confronted in his home; a robbery suspect. He did manage to get Ada to Boston, just as Kringle got Johnny Boyle there.

That was the last I heard. I never did find out what happened to any of them; Johnny, Ada , Moze. Adas place is getting a little run down. Wiggins office was moved to Old Town. The wrestlers all got jobs on the WPA, as did I years later. I guess Ada and Moze both ended up being cared for the rest of their lives in some institutions. Johnny lost his contract with Breyhausser that year, and by the time he got done handing out his money and paying everyones hospital bills, he had no money left for himself. There wasn't a doctor in Boston that would look at him. His hand became useless. Some even say it got gangrene. Anyway, that was the end of his cooking days. I wished I had picked Boston to travel to on this birthday. I wanted to search for Johnny.

I walked over to 'Black Mac', which was rusting over a little, and lit a small fire. I threw in the dominos to burn, but I kept one. I also kept the sign. I looked at the pencils with the etched initials, J.B., and thought of what they stood for; Jacko Breyhausser or Johnny Boyle. I threw them into the fire.

No one seems to know what ever happened to J.B. on the streets of Boston. Like I say, the last anyone heard, he was seen selling pencils with a big rag on his hand. The city records got him listed as dead and buried in a cemetery in Swampscott.

I eventually ended up marrying Val, and we moved to Springfield, Massachusetts to work in the rifle factories of Smith and Wesson. On our way down there, we passed through Boston on the old post road, and kept our eyes open, just in case we came across an old one- armed Irishman selling pencils. We eventually found our way back to southern Maine, Wells to be exact, raised a family and opened our own Indian Moccasin Shop, where we still barter with the tourists. I sew the moccasins, Val does the beadwork. For years I kept my pact with Johnny, never telling anyone about the dead fish.

Today, I tell my grandkids the story of Johnny Boyle. He would want it to be told. Not just some things, but everything. As seasons change, ice doesn't melt in Maine, ice goes out.

Some things have changed; the Penobscot Exchange is gone, the lumber industry is not what it used to be, blacks have come a long way.

Some things don't change; the Penobscots are still fighting to get the river cleaned;

I still love baseball; when the mercury rises, the ice goes out.

About the Author

Danl Lane is a Penobscot Native living in the great state of Maine. Originally from Springfield, Massachusetts, he graduated from Springfield Technical with an associates Degree in Telecommunications. He went on to write for several newspapers before his ancestry was longing him back. After settling in Maine for good, he finally found the time to write Ice Goes Out, a collection of true tales woven into a fictitious story. He is also an accomplished musician, having written over 100 songs, and has one CD to his credit. He has also penned the comedy play, A Honeymooners Holiday. Danl is an avid sports fan, will always live near the ocean, and has a deep appreciation for flora and fauna.

About the illustrator

Thomas Dahill was born in Cambridge, Mass. and raised in Arlington. After receiving a degree in Chemistry at Tufts, he went on to study at the School of the Museum of Fine Arts in Boston, graduating in Painting. He was awarded a fellowship to the American Academy in Rome. Tom taught at the Museum of Fine Arts and Emerson College, where he was chairman of the Fine Arts Dept. His paintings and drawings have been exhibited in Boston and abroad. His most recent illustrations can be found in "Cambridge on the Charles", "The Incredible Ditch" and several volumes of poetry. Tom is a well traveled veteran with many war stories.

Printed in the United States
138452LV00002B/448/A